D1449544

TOLKIEN'S WORLD

TOLKIEN

TOLKIEN'S WORLD

Paintings of Middle-Earth

MJF BOOKS   New York

Each of the individual illustrations in this book is reproduced by permission of the copyright holders: Inger Edelfeldt, Michael Hague, John Howe, Anthony Galuidi, Roger Garland, Robert Goldsmith, Alan Lee, Ted Nasmith, Carol Emery Phenix.

Text quotations are from the following sources:
The Hobbit by J. R. R. Tolkien © George Allen & Unwin (Publishers) Ltd 1937, 1951, 1966, 1978
The Fellowship of the Ring by J. R. R. Tolkien © George Allen & Unwin (Publishers) Ltd 1954, 1966
The Two Towers by J. R. R. Tolkien © George Allen & Unwin (Publishers) Ltd 1954, 1966
The Return of the King by J. R. R. Tolkien © George Allen & Unwin (Publishers) Ltd 1955, 1966
The Silmarillion by J. R. R. Tolkien © George Allen & Unwin (Publishers) Ltd 1977. 1979, 1983
The Book of Lost Tales Volume One by J. R. R. Tolkien © George Allen & Unwin (Publishers) Ltd 1983, 1985
The Book of Lost Tales Volume Two by J. R. R. Tolkien © George Allen & Unwin (Publishers) Ltd 1984, 1986
The Smith of Wootton Major by J. R. R. Tolkien © George Allen & Unwin (Publishers) Ltd 1967, 1975, 1990
The Lost Road by J. R. R. Tolkien © Unwin Hyman Ltd, 1987, 1989
The Return of the Shadow by J. R. R. Tolkien © Unwin Hyman Ltd 1988, 1990

Published by MJF Books
Fine Communications
Two Lincoln Square
60 West 66th Street
New York, NY 10023

Library of Congress Catalog Card Number 97-75621
ISBN 1-56731-248-9

Copyright © HarperCollins 1992

This edition published by arrangement with HarperCollins Publishers

Printed in Italy

MJF Books and the MJF colophon are trademarks of Fine Creative Media, Inc.

10   9   8   7   6   5   4   3

Contents

John Ronald Reuel Tolkien was born on 3rd January 1892 at Bloemfontein in the Orange Free State, but at the age of four he was taken by his mother, Mary Suffield, together with his younger brother, Hilary, back to England for 'home leave'. After his father's death from rheumatic fever, the family made their home at Sarehole, on the south-eastern edge of Birmingham. Ronald spent a happy childhood in the Sarehole countryside, and his sensibility to the rural landscape can clearly be seen both in his writing and in his pictures.

After his mother's death, when Ronald was twelve, he and Hilary became wards of a kindly priest at the Birmingham Oratory. They both attended King Edward's School, Birmingham, where Ronald achieved distinction in Classics, and also encountered Anglo-Saxon and Middle English. At this time also, he began to develop his linguistic abilities by inventing languages which he related to 'fairy' or 'elvish' people.

After taking a First in English Language and Literature at Exeter College, Oxford, Tolkien married Edith Bratt, with whom he had formed an attachment when they both lived in the same lodging-house in Birmingham. He was also commissioned in the Lancashire Fusiliers and served in the battle of the Somme, where two of his three closest friends were killed.

After the war, he obtained a post on the New English Dictionary, and began to write the mythological and legendary cycle which he originally called 'The Book of Lost Tales' but which eventually became known as *The Silmarillion*.

In 1920 Tolkien, now with two children, was appointed as Reader in the English Language at the University of Leeds, a post that was converted to a Professorship four years later. He distinguished himself by his lively and imaginative teaching, and in 1925 was elected Rawlinson and Bosworth Professor of Anglo-Saxon at Oxford, where he worked with great skill and enthusiasm for many years. Indeed he was one of the most accomplished philologists that has ever been known. Meanwhile, his family, now numbering four children, encouraged Tolkien to use his mythological imagination to deal with more homely topics. For them he wrote and illustrated *The Father Christmas Letters*, and to them he told the story of *The Hobbit*, published some years later in 1937 by Stanley Unwin, who then asked for a 'sequel'. At first, Tolkien applied himself only unwillingly to this task, but soon he was inspired, and what he had meant to be another book for children grew into *The Lord of the Rings*, truly a sequel to *The Silmarillion* than to *The Hobbit*. This huge story took twelve years to complete, and it was not published until Tolkien was approaching retirement. When it did reach print, its extraordinary popularity took him by surprise.

After retirement, Tolkien and his wife lived first in the Headington area of Oxford, then moved to Bournemouth, but after his wife's death in 1971, Tolkien returned to Oxford and died after a very brief illness on 2nd September 1973, leaving his great mythological and legendary cycle *The Silmarillion* to be edited for publication by his son, Christopher.

RIVENDELL

Ted Nasmith

They saw a valley far below. They could hear the voice of hurrying water in a rocky bed at the bottom; the scent of trees was in the air; and there was a light on the valley-side across the water.

Bilbo never forgot the way they slithered and slipped in the dusk down the steep zig-zag path into the secret valley of Rivendell. The air grew warmer as they got lower, and the smell of the pine-trees made him drowsy, so that every now and again he nodded and nearly fell off, or bumped his nose on the pony's neck. Their spirits rose as they went down and down. The trees changed to beech and oak, and there was a comfortable feeling in the twilight. The last green had almost faded out of the grass, when they came at length to an open glade not far above the banks of the stream.

The Hobbit

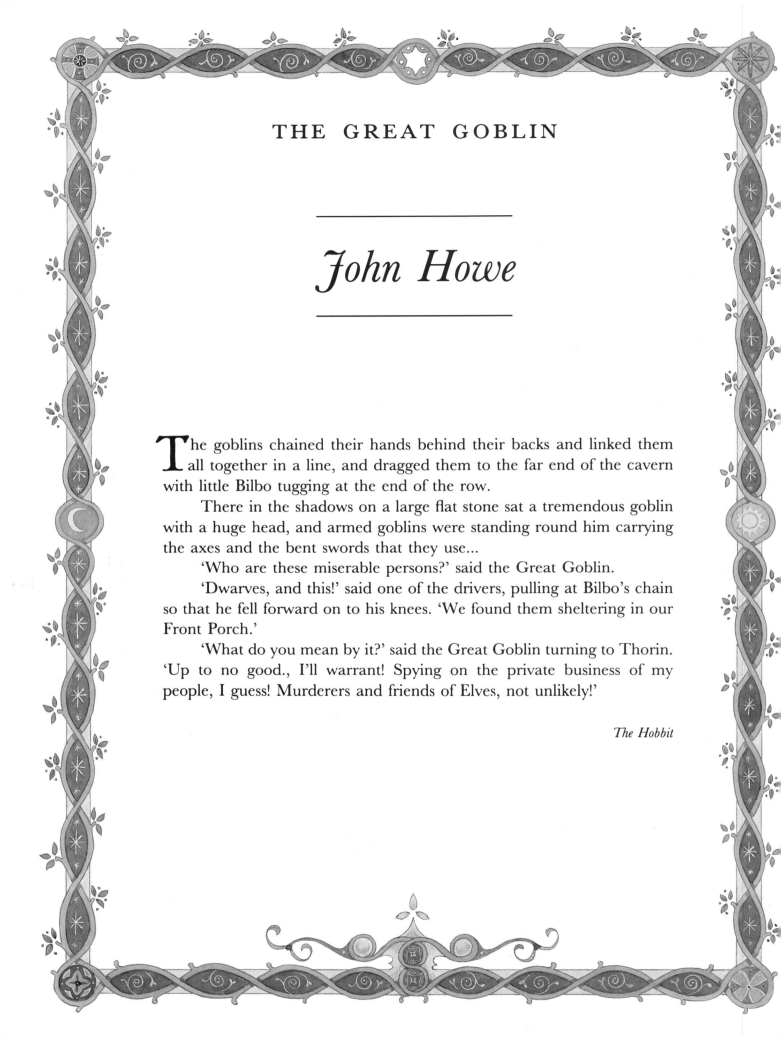

THE GREAT GOBLIN

John Howe

The goblins chained their hands behind their backs and linked them all together in a line, and dragged them to the far end of the cavern with little Bilbo tugging at the end of the row.

There in the shadows on a large flat stone sat a tremendous goblin with a huge head, and armed goblins were standing round him carrying the axes and the bent swords that they use...

'Who are these miserable persons?' said the Great Goblin.

'Dwarves, and this!' said one of the drivers, pulling at Bilbo's chain so that he fell forward on to his knees. 'We found them sheltering in our Front Porch.'

'What do you mean by it?' said the Great Goblin turning to Thorin. 'Up to no good., I'll warrant! Spying on the private business of my people, I guess! Murderers and friends of Elves, not unlikely!'

The Hobbit

GOLLUM

Inger Edelfeldt

Deep down here by the dark water lived old Gollum, a small slimy creature. I don't know where he came from, nor who or what he was. He was Gollum – as dark as darkness, except for two big round pale eyes in his thin face. He had a little boat, and he rowed about quite quietly on the lake; for lake it was, wide and deep and deadly cold. He paddled it with large feet dangling over the side, but never a ripple did he make. Not he. He was looking out of his pale lamp-like eyes for blind fish, which he grabbed with his long fingers as quick as thinking. He liked meat too. Goblin he thought good, when he could get it; but he took every care they never found him out. He just throttled them from behind, if they ever came down alone anywhere near the edge of the water, while he was prowling about.

The Hobbit

Michael Hague

A box without hinges, key, or lid,
But golden treasure inside is hid,

he asked to gain time, until he could think of a really hard one. This he thought a dreadfully easy chestnut, though he had not asked it in the usual words. But it proved a nasty poser for Gollum. He hissed to himself, and still he did not answer; he whispered and spluttered.

After some while Bilbo became impatient. 'Well, what is it?' he said. 'The answer's not a kettle boiling over, as you seem to think from the noise you are making.'

'Give us a chance; let it give us a chance, my preciouss-ss-ss.'

'Well,' said Bilbo after giving him a long chance, 'what about your guess?'

But suddenly Gollum remembered thieving from nests long ago, and sitting under the river bank teaching his grandmother, teaching his grandmother to suck—'Eggses!' he hissed. 'Eggses it is!'

The Hobbit

RESCUED BY EAGLES

Michael Hague

Then Gandalf climbed to the top of his tree. The sudden splendour flashed from his wand like lightning, as he got ready to spring down from on high right among the spears of the goblins. That would have been the end of him, though he would probably have killed many of them as he came hurtling down like a thunderbolt. But he never leaped.

Just at that moment the Lord of the Eagles swept down from above, seized him in his talons, and was gone.

There was a howl of anger and surprise from the goblins. Loud cried the Lord of the Eagles, to whom Gandalf had now spoken. Back swept the great birds that were with him, and down they came like huge black shadows. The wolves yammered and gnashed their teeth; the goblins yelled and stamped with rage, and flung their heavy spears in the air in vain.

The Hobbit

FLYING WITH THE EAGLES

Michael Hague

This time he was allowed to climb on to an eagle's back and cling between his wings. The air rushed over him and he shut his eyes. The dwarves were crying farewells and promising to repay the Lord of the Eagles if ever they could, as off rose fifteen great birds from the mountain's side. The sun was still close to the eastern edge of things. The morning was cool, and mists were in the valleys and hollows and twined here and there about the peaks and pinnacles of the hills. Bilbo opened an eye to peep and saw that the birds were already high up and the world was far away, and the mountains were falling back behind them into the distance.

The Hobbit

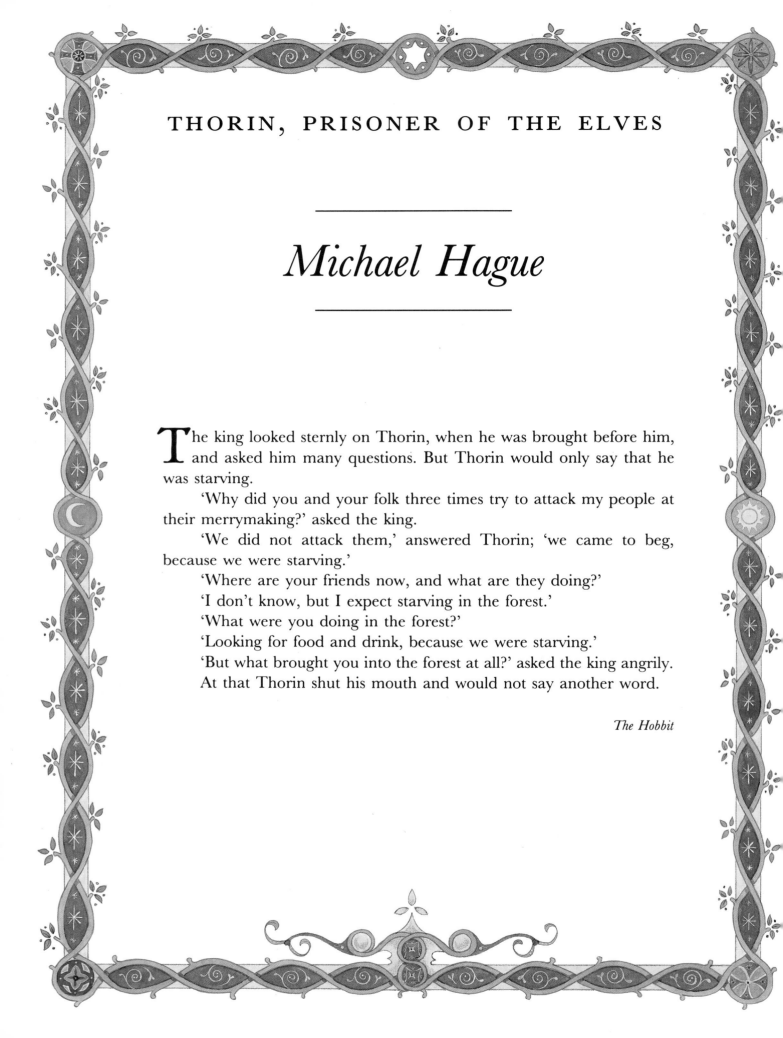

Michael Hague

The king looked sternly on Thorin, when he was brought before him, and asked him many questions. But Thorin would only say that he was starving.

'Why did you and your folk three times try to attack my people at their merrymaking?' asked the king.

'We did not attack them,' answered Thorin; 'we came to beg, because we were starving.'

'Where are your friends now, and what are they doing?'

'I don't know, but I expect starving in the forest.'

'What were you doing in the forest?'

'Looking for food and drink, because we were starving.'

'But what brought you into the forest at all?' asked the king angrily.

At that Thorin shut his mouth and would not say another word.

The Hobbit

Carol Emery Phenix

There he lay, a vast red-golden dragon, fast asleep; a thrumming came from his jaws and nostrils, and wisps of smoke, but his fires were low in slumber. Beneath him, under all his limbs and his huge coiled tail, and about him on all sides stretching away across the unseen floors, lay countless piles of precious things, gold wrought and unwrought, gems and jewels, and silver red-stained in the ruddy light.

The Hobbit

SMAUG THE MAGNIFICENT

Michael Hague

He stirred and stretched forth his neck to sniff. Then he missed the cup! Thieves! Fire! Murder! Such a thing had not happened since he first came to the Mountain! His rage passes description – the sort of rage that is only seen when rich folk that have more than they can enjoy suddenly lose something that they have long had but have never before used or wanted. His fire belched forth, the hall smoked, he shook the mountain-roots. He thrust his head in vain at the little hole, and then coiling his length together, roaring like thunder underground, he sped from his deep lair through its great door, out into the huge passages of the mountain-palace and up towards the Front Gate.

The Hobbit

THE BLACK ARROW

Michael Hague

Suddenly out of the dark something fluttered to his shoulder. He started but it was only an old thrush. Unafraid it perched by his ear and it brought him news. Marvelling he found he could understand its tongue, for he was of the race of Dale.

'Wait! Wait!' it said to him. 'The moon is rising. Look for the hollow of the left breast as he flies and turns above you!'

And while Bard paused in wonder it told him of tidings up in the Mountain and of all that it had heard.

Then Bard drew his bow-string to his ear. The dragon was circling back, flying low, and as he came the moon rose above the eastern shore and silvered his great wings.

'Arrow!' said the bowman. 'Black arrow! I have saved you to the last. You have never failed me and always I have recovered you. I had you from my father and he from of old. If ever you came from the forges of the true king under the Mountain, go now and speed well!'

Hobbit

SMAUG OVER ESGAROTH

John Howe

Fire leaped from the dragon's jaws. He circled for a while high in the air above them lighting all the lake; the trees by the shores shone like copper and like blood with leaping shadows of dense black at their feet. Then down he swooped straight through the arrow-storm, reckless in his rage, taking no heed to turn his scaly sides towards his foes, seeking only to set their town alight.

Fire leaped from thatched roofs and wooden beam-ends as he hurtled down and past and round again, though all had been drenched with water before he came. Once more water was flung by a hundred hands wherever a spark appeared. Back swirled the dragon. A sweep of his tail and the roof of the Great House crumbled and smashed down. Flames unquenchable sprang high into the night.

The Hobbit

THE ARKENSTONE

Michael Hague

He drew forth the Arkenstone, and threw away the wrapping.

The Elvenking himself, whose eyes were used to things of wonder and beauty, stood up in amazement. Even Bard gazed marvelling at it in silence. It was as if a globe had been filled with moonlight and hung before them in a net woven of the glint of frosty stars.

'This is the Arkenstone of Thrain,' said Bilbo, 'the Heart of the Mountain; and it is also the heart of Thorin. He values it above a river of gold. I give it to you. It will aid you in your bargaining.' Then Bilbo, not without a shudder, not without a glance of longing, handed the marvellous stone to Bard, and he held it in his hand, as though dazed.

The Hobbit

Inger Edelfeldt

My *dear People*, began Bilbo, rising in his place. 'Hear! Hear! Hear!'
they shouted, and kept on repeating it in chorus, seeming reluctant
to follow their own advice. Bilbo left his place and went and stood on a
chair under the illuminated tree. The light of the lanterns fell on his
beaming face; the golden buttons shone on his embroidered silk
waistcoat. They could all see him standing, waving one hand in the air,
the other was in his trouser-pocket.

My dear Bagginses and Boffins, he began again; *and my dear Tooks and
Brandybucks, and Grubbs, and Chubbs, and Burrowses, and Hornblowers, and
Bolgers, Bracegirdles, Goodbodies, Brockhouses, and Proudfoots...Also my good
Sackville-Bagginses that I welcome back at last to Bag End. Today is my one hundred
and eleventh birthday: I am eleventy-one today!'*

The Fellowship of the Ring

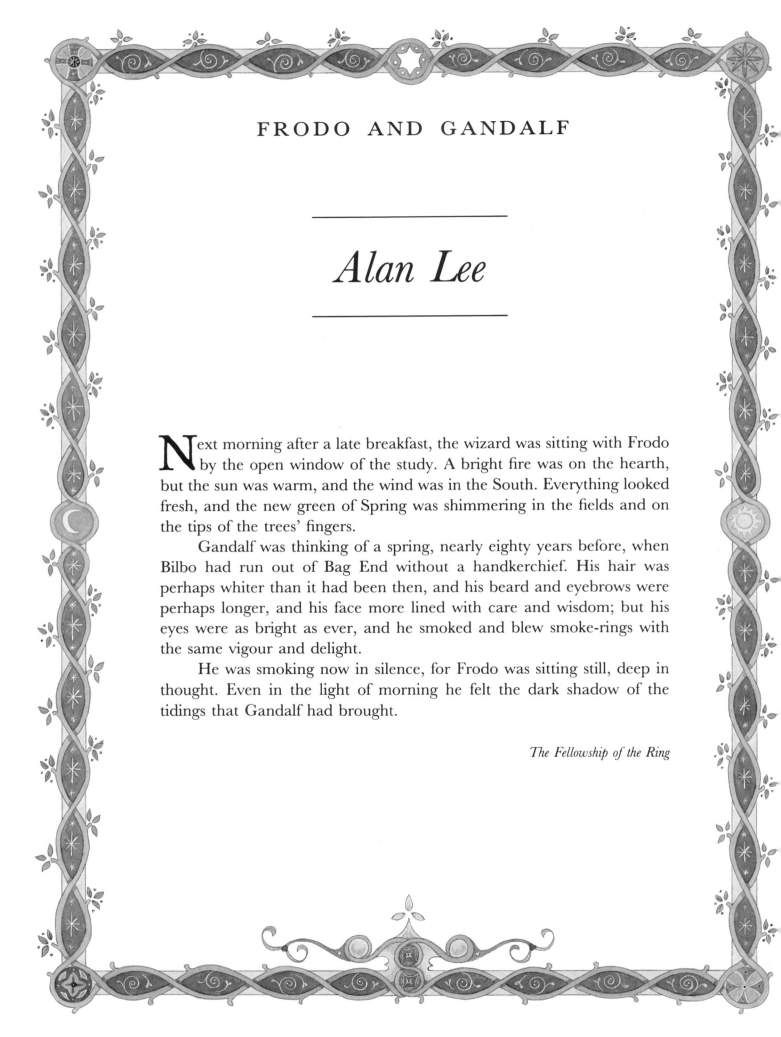

FRODO AND GANDALF

Alan Lee

Next morning after a late breakfast, the wizard was sitting with Frodo by the open window of the study. A bright fire was on the hearth, but the sun was warm, and the wind was in the South. Everything looked fresh, and the new green of Spring was shimmering in the fields and on the tips of the trees' fingers.

Gandalf was thinking of a spring, nearly eighty years before, when Bilbo had run out of Bag End without a handkerchief. His hair was perhaps whiter than it had been then, and his beard and eyebrows were perhaps longer, and his face more lined with care and wisdom; but his eyes were as bright as ever, and he smoked and blew smoke-rings with the same vigour and delight.

He was smoking now in silence, for Frodo was sitting still, deep in thought. Even in the light of morning he felt the dark shadow of the tidings that Gandalf had brought.

The Fellowship of the Ring

GREEN HILL COUNTRY

Ted Nasmith

The day's march promised to be warm and tiring work. After some miles, however, the road ceased to roll up and down: it climbed to the top of a steep bank in a weary zig-zagging sort of way, and then prepared to go down for the last time. In front of them they saw the lower lands dotted with small clumps of trees that melted away in the distance to a brown woodland haze. They were looking across the Woody End towards the Brandywine River. The road wound away before them like a piece of string.

'The road goes on for ever,' said Pippin; ' but I can't without a rest. It is high time for lunch.'

The Fellowship of the Ring

LEAVING THE SHIRE

Ted Nasmith

The leaves of the trees were glistening, and every twig was dripping; the grass was grey with cold dew. Everything was still, and far-away noises seemed near and clear: fowls chattering in a yard, someone closing a door of a distant house.

In their shed they found the ponies; sturdy little beasts of the kind loved by hobbits, not speedy, but good for a long day's work. They mounted, and soon they were riding off into the mist, which seemed to open reluctantly before them and close forbiddingly behind them. After riding for about an hour, slowly and without talking, they saw the Hedge looming suddenly ahead. It was tall and netted over with silver cobwebs.

The Fellowship of the Ring

TOM BOMBADIL

Roger Garland

Frodo and Sam stood as if enchanted. The wind puffed out. The leaves hung silently again on stiff branches. There was another burst of song, and then suddenly, hopping and dancing along the path, there appeared above the reeds an old battered hat with a tall crown and a long blue feather stuck in the band. With another hop and a bound there came into view a man, or so it seemed. At any rate he was too large and heavy for a hobbit, if not quite tall enough for one of the Big People, though he made enough noise for one, stumping along with great yellow boots on his thick legs, and charging through grass and rushes like a cow going down to drink. He had a blue coat and a long brown beard; his eyes were blue and bright, and his face was red as a ripe apple, but creased into a hundred wrinkles of laughter. In his hands he carried on a large leaf as on a tray a small pile of white water-lilies.

The Fellowship of the Ring

UNDER THE SPELL OF THE BARROW-WIGHT

Ted Nasmith

Suddenly a song began: a cold murmur, rising and falling...

> Cold be hand and heart and bone,
> and cold be sleep under stone:
> never more to wake on stony bed,
> never, till the Sun fails and the Moon is dead.
> In the black wind the stars shall die,
> and still on gold here let them lie,
> till the dark lord lifts his hand
> over dead sea and withered land.

He heard behind his head a creaking and scraping sound. Raising himself on one arm he looked, and saw now in the pale light that they were in a kind of passage which behind them turned a corner. Round the corner a long arm was groping, walking on its fingers towards Sam, who was lying nearest, and towards the hilt of the sword that lay upon him.

The Fellowship of the Ring

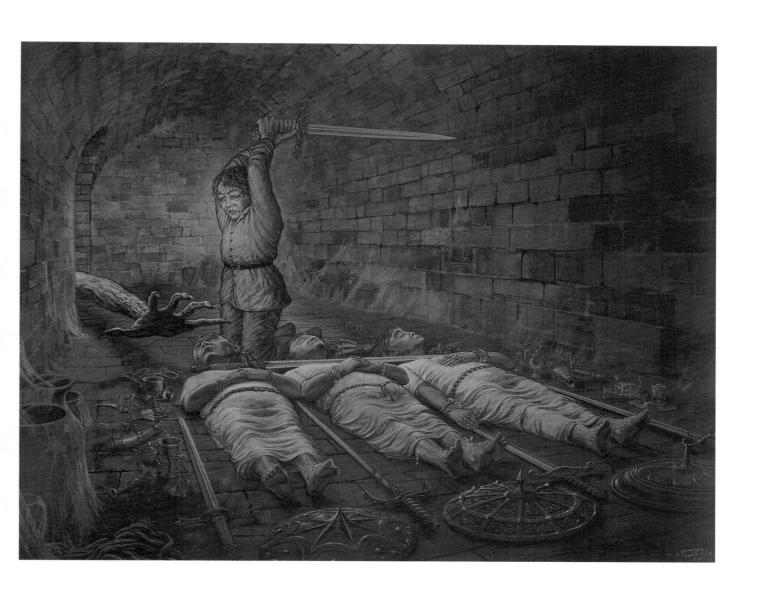

LÚTHIEN TINÚVIEL

Alan Lee

*T*he leaves were long, the grass was green,
  The hemlock-umbels tall and fair,
And in the glade a light was seen
  Of stars in shadow shimmering.
Tinúviel was dancing there
  To music of a pipe unseen,
And light of stars was in her hair,
  And in her raiment glimmering.

There Beren came from mountains cold,
  And lost he wandered under leaves,
And where the Elven-river rolled
  He walked alone and sorrowing.
He peered between the hemlock-leaves
  And saw in wonder flowers of gold
Upon her mantle and her sleeves,
  And her hair like shadow following.

The Fellowship of the Ring

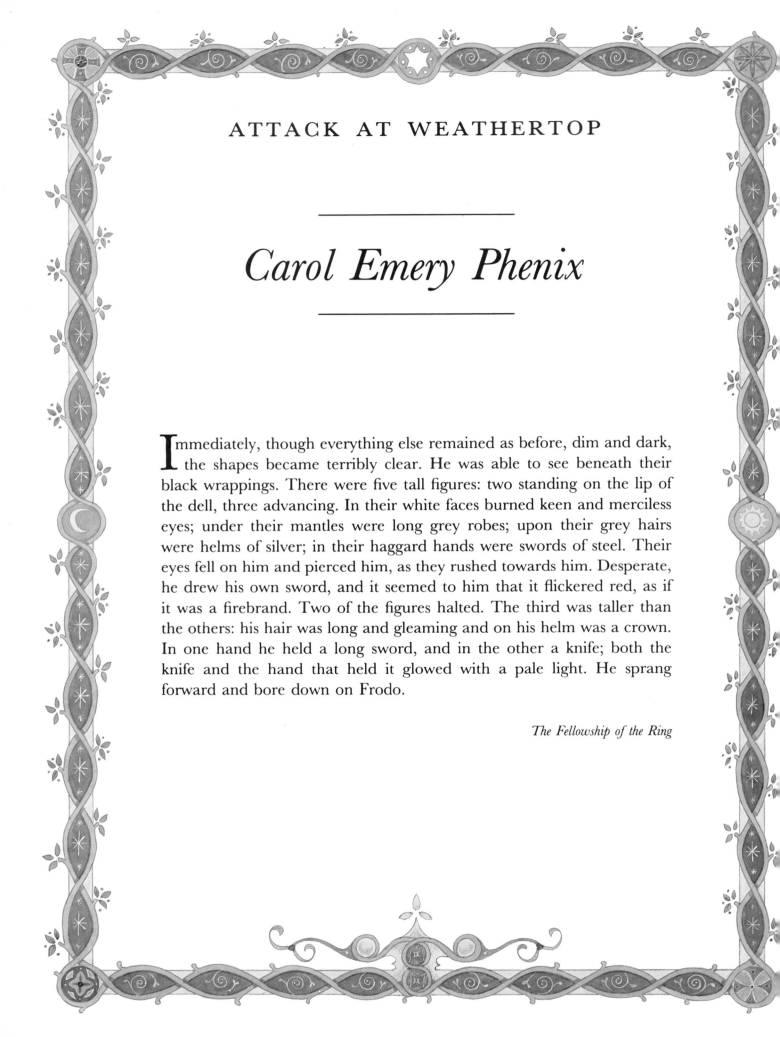

Carol Emery Phenix

Immediately, though everything else remained as before, dim and dark, the shapes became terribly clear. He was able to see beneath their black wrappings. There were five tall figures: two standing on the lip of the dell, three advancing. In their white faces burned keen and merciless eyes; under their mantles were long grey robes; upon their grey hairs were helms of silver; in their haggard hands were swords of steel. Their eyes fell on him and pierced him, as they rushed towards him. Desperate, he drew his own sword, and it seemed to him that it flickered red, as if it was a firebrand. Two of the figures halted. The third was taller than the others: his hair was long and gleaming and on his helm was a crown. In one hand he held a long sword, and in the other a knife; both the knife and the hand that held it glowed with a pale light. He sprang forward and bore down on Frodo.

The Fellowship of the Ring

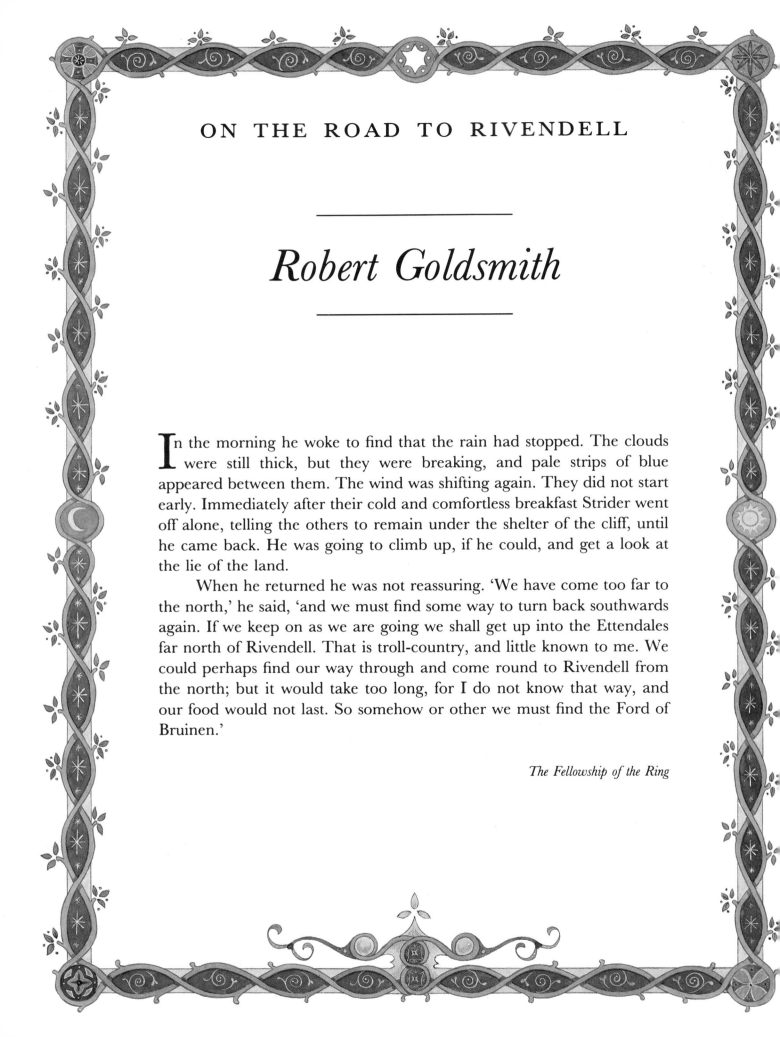

ON THE ROAD TO RIVENDELL

Robert Goldsmith

In the morning he woke to find that the rain had stopped. The clouds were still thick, but they were breaking, and pale strips of blue appeared between them. The wind was shifting again. They did not start early. Immediately after their cold and comfortless breakfast Strider went off alone, telling the others to remain under the shelter of the cliff, until he came back. He was going to climb up, if he could, and get a look at the lie of the land.

When he returned he was not reassuring. 'We have come too far to the north,' he said, 'and we must find some way to turn back southwards again. If we keep on as we are going we shall get up into the Ettendales far north of Rivendell. That is troll-country, and little known to me. We could perhaps find our way through and come round to Rivendell from the north; but it would take too long, for I do not know that way, and our food would not last. So somehow or other we must find the Ford of Bruinen.'

The Fellowship of the Ring

THE STONE TROLLS

Alan Lee

The sun was now high, and it shone down through the half-stripped branches of the trees, and lit the clearing with bright patches of light. They halted suddenly on the edge, and peered through the tree-trunks, holding their breath. There stood the trolls: three large trolls. One was stooping, and the other two stood staring at him.

Strider walked forward unconcernedly. 'Get up, old stone!' he said, and broke his stick upon the stooping troll.

Nothing happened. There was a gasp of astonishment from the hobbits, and then even Frodo laughed. 'Well!' he said. 'We are forgetting our family history! These must be the very three that were caught by Gandalf, quarrelling over the right way to cook thirteen dwarves and one hobbit.'

The Fellowship of the Ring

Ted Nasmith

'By Elbereth and Lúthien the Fair,' said Frodo with a last effort, lifting up his sword, 'you shall have neither the Ring nor me!'

Then the leader, who was now half across the Ford, stood up menacing in his stirrups, and raised up his hand. Frodo was stricken dumb. He felt his tongue cleave to his mouth, and his heart labouring. The sword broke and fell out of his shaking hand. The elf-horse reared and snorted. The foremost of the black horses had almost set foot upon the shore.

At that moment there came a roaring and a rushing: a noise of loud waters rolling many stones. Dimly Frodo saw the river below him rise, and down along its course there came a plumed cavalry of waves. White flames seemed to Frodo to flicker on their crests and he half fancied that he saw amid the water white riders upon white horses with frothing manes.

The Fellowship of the Ring

SARUMAN

Tony Galuidi

" 'The Nine have come forth again,' I answered. 'They have crossed the River. So Radagast said to me.'

" ' 'Radagast the Brown!' laughed Saruman, and he no longer concealed his scorn. 'Radagast the Bird-tamer! Radagast the Simple! Radagast the Fool! Yet he had just the wit to play the part that I set him. For you have come, and that was all the purpose of my message. And here you will stay, Gandalf the Grey, and rest from journeys. For I am Saruman the Wise, Saruman Ring-maker, Saruman of Many Colours!' "

The Fellowship of the Ring

Ted Nasmith

They passed through the lane; but hardly had Frodo touched the ground when a deep rumble there rolled down a fall of stones and slithering snow. The spray of it half blinded the Company as they crouched against the cliff, and when the air had cleared again they saw the path was blocked behind them.

'Enough, enough!' cried Gimli. 'We are departing as quickly as we may!' And indeed with that last stroke the malice of the mountain seemed to be expended, as if Caradhras was satisfied that the invaders had been beaten off and would not dare to return.

The Fellowship of the Ring

THE ENTRANCE TO MORIA

Alan Lee

A mile southwards along the shore they came upon holly trees. Stumps and dead boughs were rotting in the shadows, the remains it seemed of old thickets, or of a hedge that had once lined the road across the drowned valley. But close under the cliff there stood, still strong and living, two tall trees, larger than any trees of holly that Frodo had ever seen or imagined. Their great roots spread from the wall to the water. Under the looming cliffs they had looked like mere bushes, when seen far off from the top of the Stair; but now they towered overhead, stiff, dark and silent, throwing deep night-shadows about their feet, standing like sentinel pillars at the end of the road.

'Well, here we are at last!' said Gandalf. 'Here the Elven-way from Hollin ended. Holly was the token of the people of that land, and they planted it here to mark the end of their domain; for the West-door was made chiefly for their use in their traffic with the Lords of Moria. Those were happier days, when there was still close friendship at times between folk of different race, even between Dwarves and Elves.'

The Fellowship of the Ring

GANDALF

John Howe

When evening in the Shire was grey
his footsteps on the Hill were heard;
before the dawn he went away
on journey long without a word.

From Wilderland to Western shore,
from northern waste to southern hill,
through dragon-lair and hidden door
and darkling woods he walked at will.

The Fellowship of the Ring

GALADRIEL'S MIRROR

Alan Lee

Down a long flight of steps the Lady went into a deep green hollow, through which ran murmuring the silver stream that issued from the fountain on the hill. At the bottom, upon a low pedestal carved like a branching tree, stood a basin of silver, wide and shallow, and beside it stood a silver ewer.

With water from the stream Galadriel filled the basin to the brim, and breathed on it, and when the water was still again she spoke. 'Here is the Mirror of Galadriel,' she said. 'I have brought you here so that you may look in it, if you will.'

The air was very still, and the dell was dark, and the Elf-lady beside him was tall and pale. 'What shall we look for, and what shall we see?' asked Frodo, filled with awe.

The Fellowship of the Ring

TOL BRANDIR

Alan Lee

Wandering aimlessly at first in the wood, Frodo found that his feet were leading him up towards the slopes of the hill. He came to a path, the dwindling ruins of a road of long ago. In steep places stairs of stone had been hewn, but now they were cracked and worn, and split by the roots of trees. For some while he climbed, not caring which way he went, until he came to a grassy place. Rowan-trees grew about it, and in the midst was a flat wide stone. The little upland lawn was open upon the East and filled now with the early sunlight. Frodo halted and looked out over the River, far below him, to Tol Brandir and the birds wheeling in the great gulf of air between him and the untrodden isle. The voice of Rauros was a mighty roaring mingled with a deep throbbing boom.

The Fellowship of the Ring

BARAD-DÛR

Tony Galuidi

But against Minas Tirith was set another fortress, greater and more strong. Thither, eastward, unwilling his eye was drawn. It passed the ruined bridges of Osgiliath, the grinning gates of Minas Morgul, and the haunted Mountains, and it looked upon Gorgoroth, the valley of terror in the Land of Mordor. Darkness lay there under the Sun. Fire glowed amid the smoke. Mount Doom was burning, and a great reek rising. Then at last his gaze was held: wall upon wall, battlement upon battlement, black, immeasurably strong, mountain of iron, gate of steel, tower of adamant, he saw it: Barad-dûr, Fortress of Sauron. All hope left him.

The Fellowship of the Ring

Roger Garland

'You cannot pass,' he said. The orcs stood still, and a dead silence fell. I am a servant of the Secret Fire, wielder of the flame of Anor. You cannot pass. The dark fire will not avail you, flame of Udûn. Go back to the Shadow! You cannot pass.'

The Balrog made no answer. The fire in it seemed to die, but the darkness grew. It stepped forward slowly on to the bridge, and suddenly it drew itself up to a great height, and its wings were spread from wall to wall; but still Gandalf could be seen, glimmering in the gloom; he seemed small, and altogether alone: grey and bent, like a wizened tree before the onset of a storm.

From out of the shadow a red sword leapt flaming.

Glamdring glittered white in answer.

There was a ringing clash and a stab of white fire. The Balrog fell back and its sword flew up in molten fragments. The wizard swayed on the bridge, stepped back a pace, and then again stood still.

The Fellowship of the Ring

THE BALROG

Ted Nasmith

With a bound the Balrog leaped full upon the bridge. Its whip whirled and hissed.

'He cannot stand alone!' cried Aragorn suddenly and ran back along the bridge. 'Elendil!' he shouted. 'I am with you, Gandalf!'

'Gondor!' cried Boromir and leaped after him.

At that moment Gandalf lifted his staff, and crying aloud he smote the bridge before him. The staff broke asunder and fell from his hand. A blinding sheet of white flame sprang up. The bridge cracked. Right at the Balrog's feet it broke, and the stone upon which it stood crashed into the gulf, while the rest remained, poised, quivering like a tongue of rock thrust out into emptiness.

The Fellowship of the Ring

THE LAST WORDS
OF BOROMIR

Ted Nasmith

Amile, maybe, from Parth Galen in a little glade not far from the lake he found Boromir. He was sitting with his back to a great tree, as if he was resting. But Aragorn saw that he was pierced with many black-feathered arrows; his sword was still in his hand, but it was broken near the hilt; his horn cloven in two was at his side. Many Orcs lay slain, piled all about him and at his feet.

Aragorn knelt beside him. Boromir opened his eyes and strove to speak. At last slow words came. 'I tried to take the Ring from Frodo,' he said. 'I am sorry. I have paid.' His glance strayed to his fallen enemies; twenty at least lay there. 'They have gone: the Halflings: the Orcs have taken them. I think they are not dead. Orcs bound them.' He paused and his eyes closed wearily. After a moment he spoke again.

'Farewell, Aragorn! Go to Minas Tirith and save my people! I have failed.'

'No!' said Aragorn, taking his hand and kissing his brow. 'You have conquered. Few have gained such a victory. Be at peace! Minas Tirith shall not fall!'

The Two Towers

THE URUK-HAI

John Howe

'There's no time to kill them properly,' said one. 'No time for play on this trip.'

'That can't be helped,' said another. 'But why not kill them quick, kill them now? They're a cursed nuisance, and we're in a hurry. Evening's coming on, and we ought to get a move on.'

'Orders,' said a third voice in a deep growl. 'Kill all but NOT the Halflings; they are to be brought back ALIVE as quickly as possible. That's my orders.'

'What are they wanted for?' asked several voices. 'Why alive? Do they give good sport?'

'No! I heard that one of them has got something, something that's wanted for the War, some elvish plot or other. Anyway they'll both be questioned.'

'Is that all you know? Why don't we search them and find out? We might find something that we could use ourselves.'

'That is a very interesting remark,' sneered a voice, softer than the others but more evil. 'I may have to report that. The prisoners are NOT to be searched or plundered: those are my orders.'

The Two Towers

WELLINGHALL

Ted Nasmith

'Hm! Here we are!' said Treebeard, breaking his long silence. 'I have brought you about seventy thousand ent-strides, but what that comes to in the measurement of your land I do not know. Anyhow we are near the roots of the Last Mountain. Part of the name of this place might be Wellinghall, if it were turned into your language. I like it. We will stay here tonight.' He set them down on the grass between the aisles of the trees, and they followed him towards the great arch...

For a moment Treebeard stood under the rain of the falling spring, and took a deep breath; then he laughed, and passed inside.

A great stone table stood there, but no chairs. At the back of the bay it was already quite dark. Treebeard lifted two great vessels and stood them on the table. They seemed to be filled with water; but he held his hands over them, and immediately they began to glow, one with a golden and the other with a rich green light; and the blending of the two lights lit the bay, as if the sun of summer was shining through a roof of young leaves.

The Two Towers

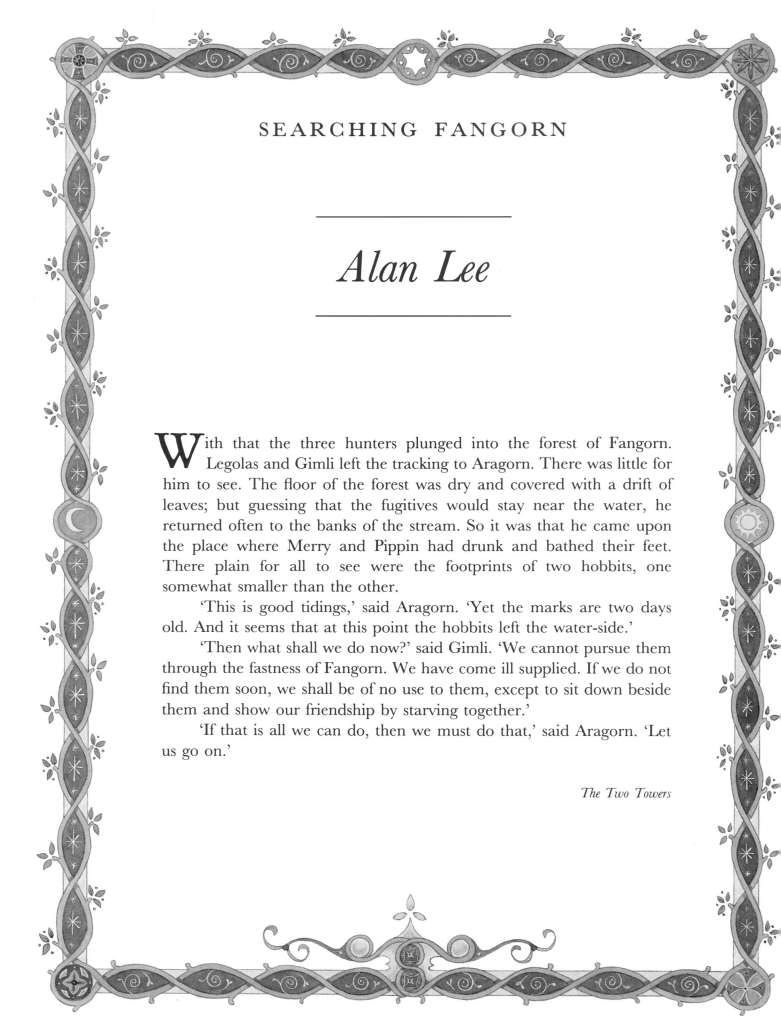

SEARCHING FANGORN

Alan Lee

With that the three hunters plunged into the forest of Fangorn. Legolas and Gimli left the tracking to Aragorn. There was little for him to see. The floor of the forest was dry and covered with a drift of leaves; but guessing that the fugitives would stay near the water, he returned often to the banks of the stream. So it was that he came upon the place where Merry and Pippin had drunk and bathed their feet. There plain for all to see were the footprints of two hobbits, one somewhat smaller than the other.

'This is good tidings,' said Aragorn. 'Yet the marks are two days old. And it seems that at this point the hobbits left the water-side.'

'Then what shall we do now?' said Gimli. 'We cannot pursue them through the fastness of Fangorn. We have come ill supplied. If we do not find them soon, we shall be of no use to them, except to sit down beside them and show our friendship by starving together.'

'If that is all we can do, then we must do that,' said Aragorn. 'Let us go on.'

The Two Towers

LEGOLAS

Inger Edelfeldt

'Legolas Greenleaf long under tree
In joy hast thou lived. Beware of the Sea!
If thou hearest the cry of the gull on the shore,
Thy heart shall then rest in the forest no more.'

The Two Towers

THE GLITTERING CAVES
OF AGLAROND

Ted Nasmith

'Gems and crystals and veins of precious ore glint in the polished walls; and the light glows through folded marbles, shell-like, translucent as the living hands of Queen Galadriel. There are columns of white and saffron and dawn-rose, Legolas, fluted and twisted into dreamlike forms; they spring up from many-coloured floors to meet the glistening pendants of the roof: wings, ropes, curtains fine as frozen clouds; spears, banners, pinnacles of suspended palaces! Still lakes mirror them: a glimmering world looks up from dark pools covered with clear glass; cities, such as the mind of Durin could scarce have imagined in his sleep, stretch on through avenues and pillared courts, on into the dark recesses where no light can come. And plink! a silver drop falls, and the round wrinkles in the glass make all the towers bend and waver like weeds and corals in a grotto of the sea.'

The Two Towers

John Howe

'I took the ball and looked at it,' stammered Pippin; 'and I saw things that frightened me. And I wanted to go away, but I couldn't. And then he came and questioned me; and he looked at me, and, and that is all I remember.'

'That won't do,' said Gandalf sternly. 'What did you see, and what did you say?'...

In a low hesitating voice Pippin began again, and slowly his words grew stronger and clearer. 'I saw a dark sky, and tall battlements,' he said. 'And tiny stars. It seemed very far away and long ago, yet hard and clear. Then the stars went in and out – they were cut off by things with wings. Very big, I think, really; but in the glass they looked like bats wheeling round the tower. I thought there were nine of them. One began to fly straight towards me, getting bigger and bigger...'

The Two Towers

THE DEAD MARSHES

Inger Edelfeldt

Wrenching his hands out of the bog, he sprang back with a cry. 'There are dead things, dead faces in the water,' he said with horror. 'Dead faces!'

Gollum laughed. 'The Dead Marshes, yes, yes: that is their names,' he cackled. 'You should not look in when the candles are lit.'

'Who are they? What are they?' asked Sam shuddering, turning to Frodo, who was now behind him.

'I don't know,' said Frodo in a dreamlike voice. 'But I have seen them too. In the pools when the candles were lit. They lie in all the pools, pale faces, deep deep under the dark water. I saw them: grim faces and evil, and noble faces and sad. But all foul, all rotting, all dead.'

The Two Towers

THE OLIPHAUNT

Inger Edelfeldt

To his astonishment and terror, and lasting delight, Sam saw a vast shape crash out of the trees and come careering down the slope. Big as a house, much bigger than a house, it looked to him, a grey-clad moving hill. Fear and wonder, maybe, enlarged him in the hobbit's eyes, but the Mûmak of Harad was indeed a beast of vast bulk, and the like of him does not walk now in Middle-earth; his kin that live still in latter days are but memories of his girth and majesty. On he came, straight towards the watchers, and then swerved aside in the nick of time, passing only a few yards away, rocking the ground beneath their feet: his great legs like trees, enormous sail-like ears spread out, long snout upraised like a huge serpent about to strike, his small red eyes raging. His upturned hornlike tusks were bound with bands of gold and dripped with blood. His trappings of scarlet and gold flapped about him in heavy tatters. The ruins of what seemed a very war-tower lay upon his heaving back, smashed in his furious passage through the woods; and high upon his neck still desperately clung a tiny figure – the body of a mighty warrior, a giant among the Swertings.

The Two Towers

SAM AND SHELOB

John Howe

Now the miserable creature was right under her, for the moment out of the reach of her sting and of her claws. Her vast belly was above him with its putrid light, and the stench of it almost smote him down. Still his fury held for one more blow, and before she could sink upon him, smothering him and all his little impudence of courage, he slashed the bright elven-blade across her with desperate strength...

She yielded to the stroke, and then heaved up the great bag of her belly high above Sam's head. Poison frothed and bubbled from the wound. Now splaying her legs she drove her great bulk down on him again. Too soon. For Sam still stood upon his feet, and dropping his own sword, with both hands he held the elven-blade point upwards, fending off that ghastly roof; and so Shelob, with the driving force of her own cruel will, with strength greater than any warrior's hand, thrust herself upon a bitter spike. Deep, deep it pricked,as Sam was crushed slowly to the ground.

The Two Towers

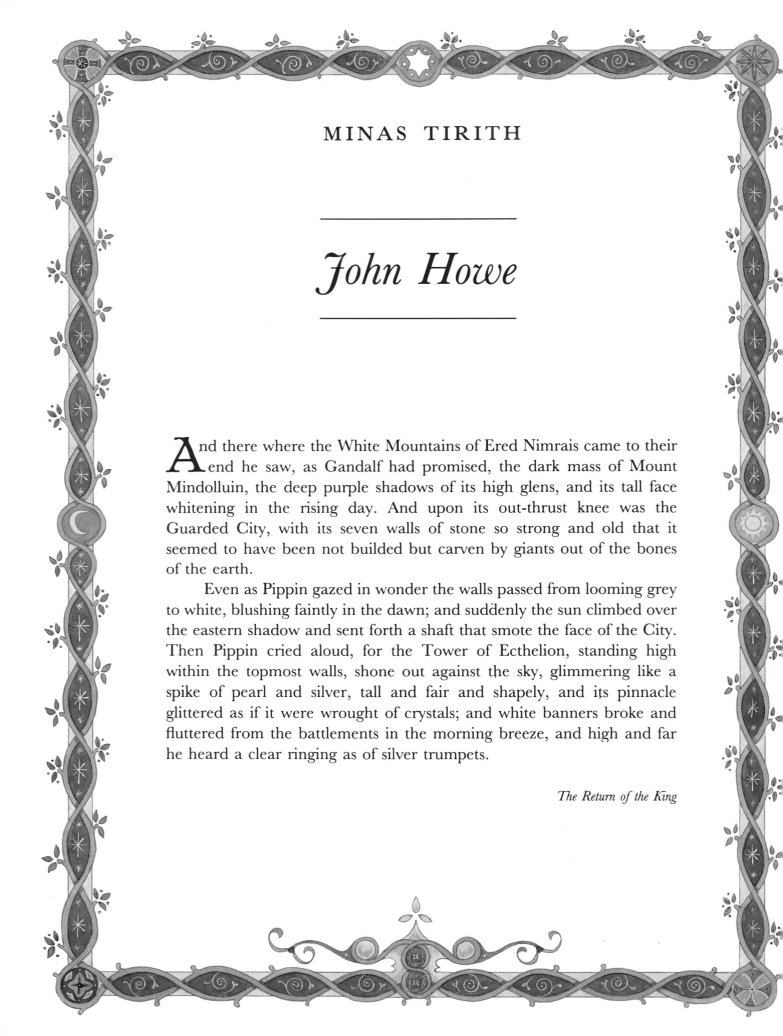

MINAS TIRITH

John Howe

And there where the White Mountains of Ered Nimrais came to their end he saw, as Gandalf had promised, the dark mass of Mount Mindolluin, the deep purple shadows of its high glens, and its tall face whitening in the rising day. And upon its out-thrust knee was the Guarded City, with its seven walls of stone so strong and old that it seemed to have been not builded but carven by giants out of the bones of the earth.

Even as Pippin gazed in wonder the walls passed from looming grey to white, blushing faintly in the dawn; and suddenly the sun climbed over the eastern shadow and sent forth a shaft that smote the face of the City. Then Pippin cried aloud, for the Tower of Ecthelion, standing high within the topmost walls, shone out against the sky, glimmering like a spike of pearl and silver, tall and fair and shapely, and its pinnacle glittered as if it were wrought of crystals; and white banners broke and fluttered from the battlements in the morning breeze, and high and far he heard a clear ringing as of silver trumpets.

The Return of the King

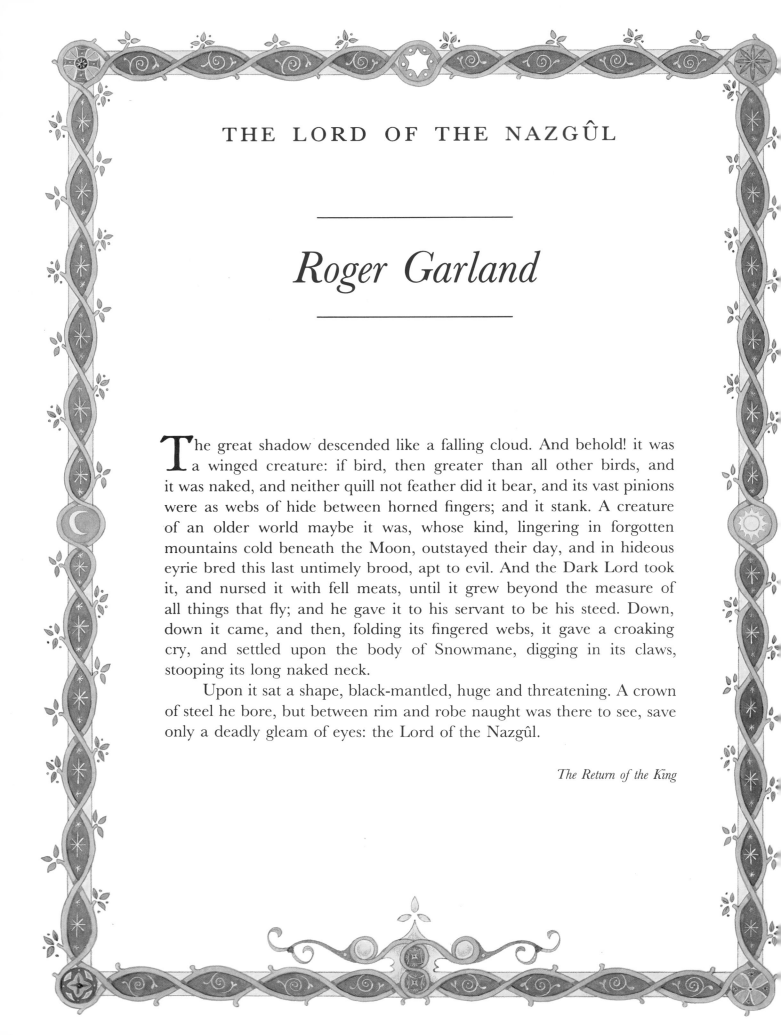

THE LORD OF THE NAZGÛL

Roger Garland

The great shadow descended like a falling cloud. And behold! it was a winged creature: if bird, then greater than all other birds, and it was naked, and neither quill not feather did it bear, and its vast pinions were as webs of hide between horned fingers; and it stank. A creature of an older world maybe it was, whose kind, lingering in forgotten mountains cold beneath the Moon, outstayed their day, and in hideous eyrie bred this last untimely brood, apt to evil. And the Dark Lord took it, and nursed it with fell meats, until it grew beyond the measure of all things that fly; and he gave it to his servant to be his steed. Down, down it came, and then, folding its fingered webs, it gave a croaking cry, and settled upon the body of Snowmane, digging in its claws, stooping its long naked neck.

Upon it sat a shape, black-mantled, huge and threatening. A crown of steel he bore, but between rim and robe naught was there to see, save only a deadly gleam of eyes: the Lord of the Nazgûl.

The Return of the King

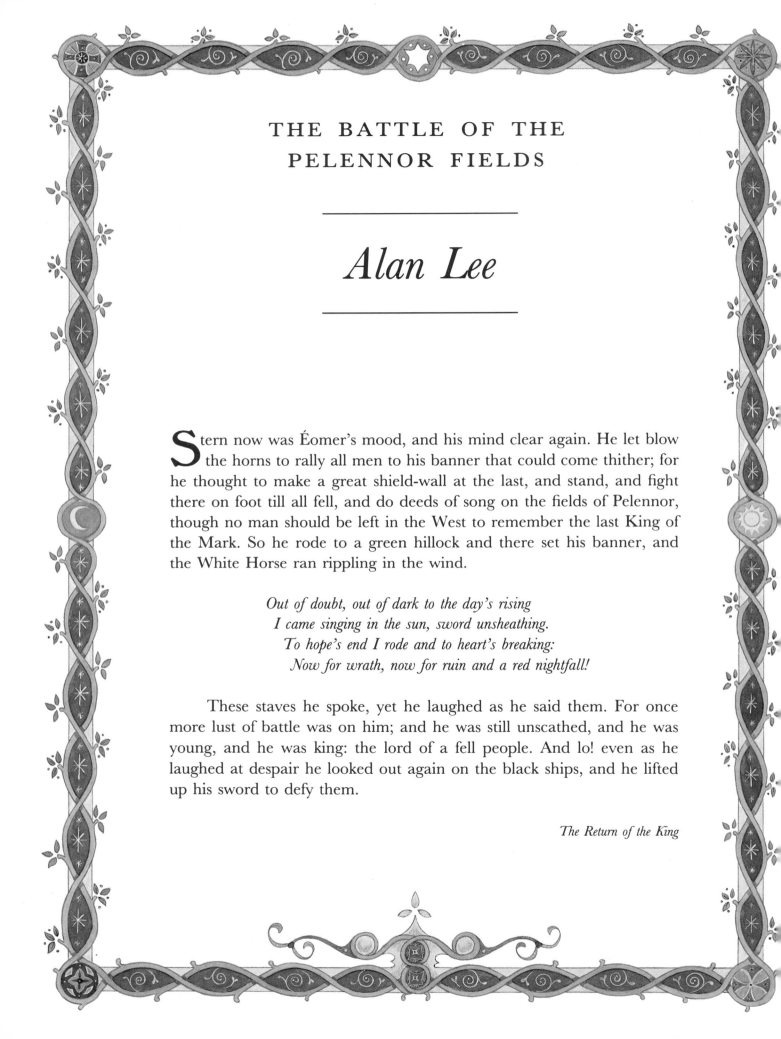

THE BATTLE OF THE
PELENNOR FIELDS

Alan Lee

Stern now was Éomer's mood, and his mind clear again. He let blow the horns to rally all men to his banner that could come thither; for he thought to make a great shield-wall at the last, and stand, and fight there on foot till all fell, and do deeds of song on the fields of Pelennor, though no man should be left in the West to remember the last King of the Mark. So he rode to a green hillock and there set his banner, and the White Horse ran rippling in the wind.

> *Out of doubt, out of dark to the day's rising*
> *I came singing in the sun, sword unsheathing.*
> *To hope's end I rode and to heart's breaking:*
> *Now for wrath, now for ruin and a red nightfall!*

These staves he spoke, yet he laughed as he said them. For once more lust of battle was on him; and he was still unscathed, and he was young, and he was king: the lord of a fell people. And lo! even as he laughed at despair he looked out again on the black ships, and he lifted up his sword to defy them.

The Return of the King

SAM IN MORDOR

Robert Goldsmith

Sam looked up towards the orc-tower, and suddenly from its narrow windows lights stared out like small red eyes. He wondered if they were some signal. His fear of the orcs, forgotten for a while in his wrath and desperation, now returned. As far as he could see, there was only one possible course for him to take: he must go on and try to find the main entrance to the dreadful tower; but his knees felt weak, and he found that he was trembling. Drawing his eyes down from the tower and the horns of the Cleft before him, he forced his unwilling feet to obey him, and slowly, listening with all his ears, peering into the dense shadows of the rocks beside the way, he retraced his steps, past the place where Frodo fell, and still the stench of Shelob lingered, and then on and on, until he stood again in the very cleft where he had put on the Ring and seen Shagrat's company go by.

The Return of the King

CIRITH UNGOL

Alan Lee

In that dreadful light Sam stood aghast, for now, looking to his left, he could see the Tower of Cirith Ungol in all its strength. The horn that he had seen from the other side was only its topmost turret. Its eastern face stood up in three great tiers from a shelf in the mountain-wall far below; its back was to a great cliff behind, from which it jutted out in pointed bastions, one above the other, diminishing as they rose, with sheer sides of cunning masonry that looked north-east and south-east. About the lowest tier, two hundred feet below where Sam now stood, there was a battlemented wall enclosing a narrow court. Its gate, upon the near south-eastern side, opened on a broad road, the outer parapet of which ran upon the brink of a precipice, until it turned southward and went winding down into the darkness to join the road that came over the Morgul Pass.

The Return of the King

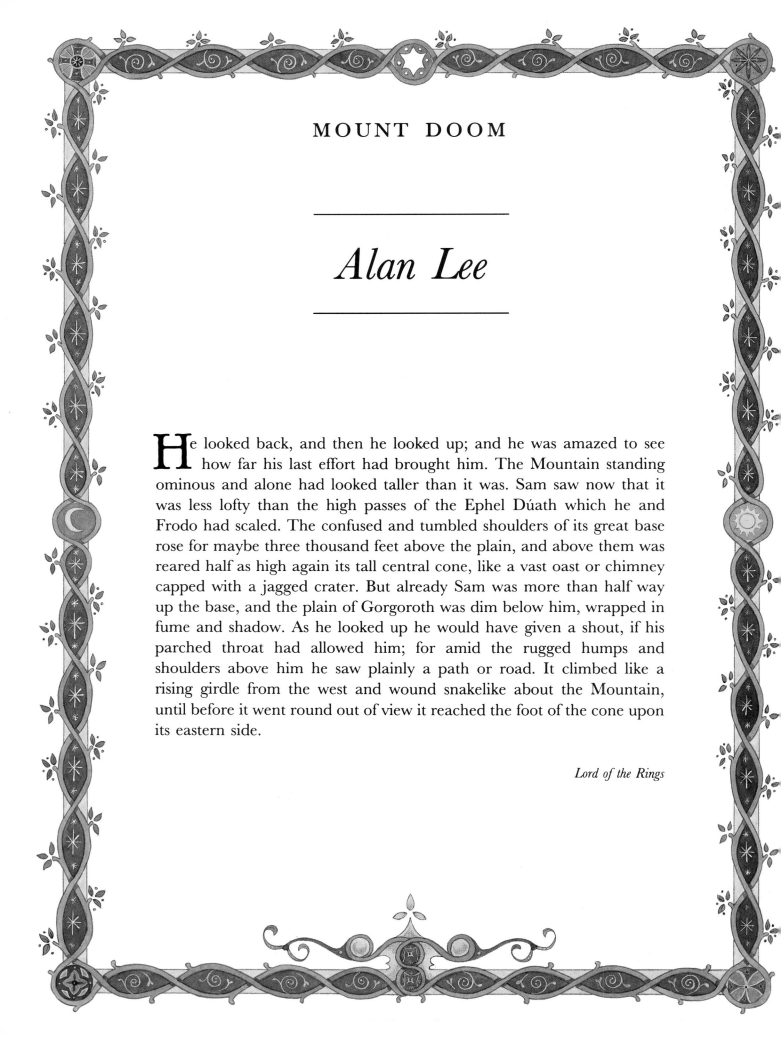

MOUNT DOOM

Alan Lee

He looked back, and then he looked up; and he was amazed to see how far his last effort had brought him. The Mountain standing ominous and alone had looked taller than it was. Sam saw now that it was less lofty than the high passes of the Ephel Dúath which he and Frodo had scaled. The confused and tumbled shoulders of its great base rose for maybe three thousand feet above the plain, and above them was reared half as high again its tall central cone, like a vast oast or chimney capped with a jagged crater. But already Sam was more than half way up the base, and the plain of Gorgoroth was dim below him, wrapped in fume and shadow. As he looked up he would have given a shout, if his parched throat had allowed him; for amid the rugged humps and shoulders above him he saw plainly a path or road. It climbed like a rising girdle from the west and wound snakelike about the Mountain, until before it went round out of view it reached the foot of the cone upon its eastern side.

Lord of the Rings

IN MORDOR

John Howe

It was hard enough for poor Sam, tired as he was; but for Frodo it was a torment, and soon a nightmare. He set his teeth and tried to stop his mind from thinking, and he struggled on. The stench of the sweating orcs about him was stifling, and he began to gasp with thirst. On, on they went, and he bent all his will to draw his breath and to make his legs keep going; and yet to what evil end he toiled and endured he did not dare to think. There was no hope of falling out unseen. Now and again the orc-driver fell back and jeered at them.

'There now!' he laughed, flicking at their legs. 'Where there's a whip there's a will, my slugs. Hold up! I'd give you a nice freshener now, only you'll get as much lash as your skins will carry when you come in late to your camp. Do you good. Don't you know we're at war?'

The Return of the King

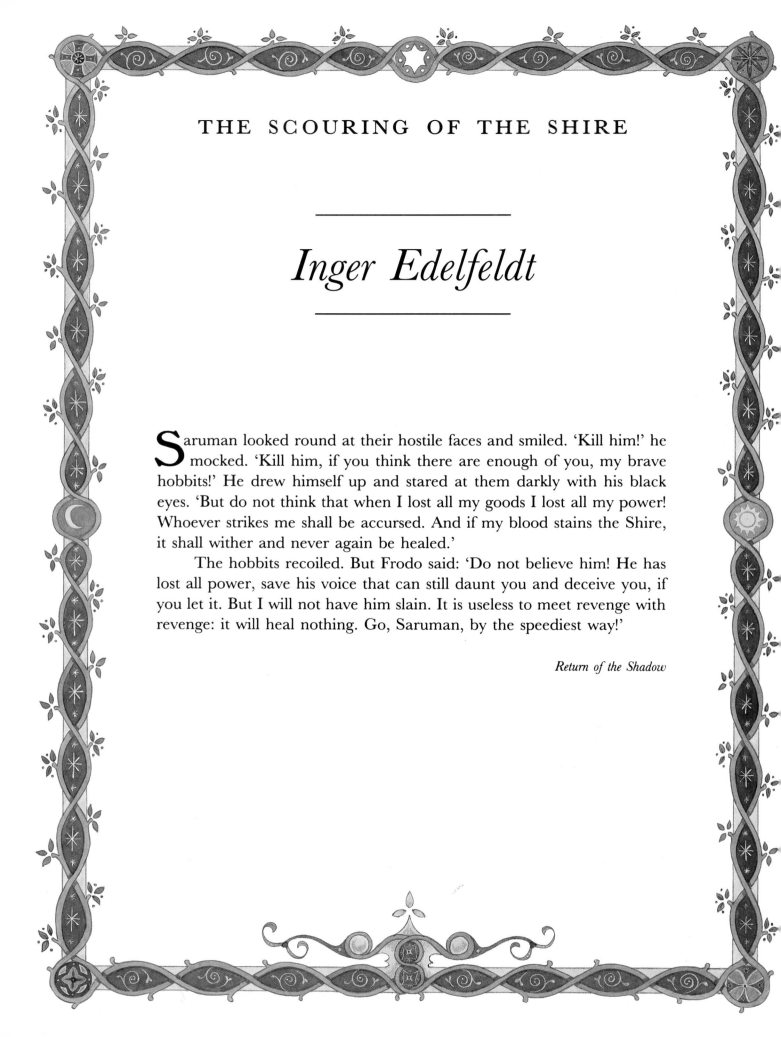

THE SCOURING OF THE SHIRE

Inger Edelfeldt

Saruman looked round at their hostile faces and smiled. 'Kill him!' he mocked. 'Kill him, if you think there are enough of you, my brave hobbits!' He drew himself up and stared at them darkly with his black eyes. 'But do not think that when I lost all my goods I lost all my power! Whoever strikes me shall be accursed. And if my blood stains the Shire, it shall wither and never again be healed.'

The hobbits recoiled. But Frodo said: 'Do not believe him! He has lost all power, save his voice that can still daunt you and deceive you, if you let it. But I will not have him slain. It is useless to meet revenge with revenge: it will heal nothing. Go, Saruman, by the speediest way!'

Return of the Shadow

Roger Garland

Ulmo is the Lord of the Waters. He is alone. He dwells nowhere long, but moves as he will in all the deep waters about the Earth or under the Earth...Ulmo loves both Elves and Men, and never abandoned them, not even when they lay under the wrath of the Valar. At times he will come unseen to the shores of Middle-earth, or pass far inland up firths of the sea, and there make music upon his great horns, the Ulumúri, that are wrought of white shell; and those to whom that music comes hear it ever after in their hearts, and longing for the sea never leaves them again. But mostly Ulmo speaks to those who dwell in Middle-earth with voices that are heard only as the music of water. For all seas, lakes, rivers, fountains and springs are in his government; so that the Elves say that the spirit of Ulmo runs in all the veins of the world.

The Silmarillion

THE CHAINING OF MELKOR

Roger Garland

Long and grievous was the siege of Utumno, and many battles were fought before its gates of which naught but the rumour is known to the Elves. In that time the shape of Middle-earth was changed, and the Great Sea that sundered it from Aman grew wide and deep; and it broke in upon the coasts and made a deep gulf to the southward...The lands of the far north were all made desolate in those days; for there Utumno was delved exceeding deep; and its pits were filled with fires and with great hosts of the servants of Melkor.

But at the last the gates of Utumno were broken and the halls unroofed, and Melkor took refuge in the uttermost pit. Then Tulkas stood forth as champion of the Valar and wrestled with him, and cast him upon his face; and he was bound with the chain Angainor that Aulë had wrought, and led captive; and the world had peace for a long age.

The Silmarillion

Roger Garland 85

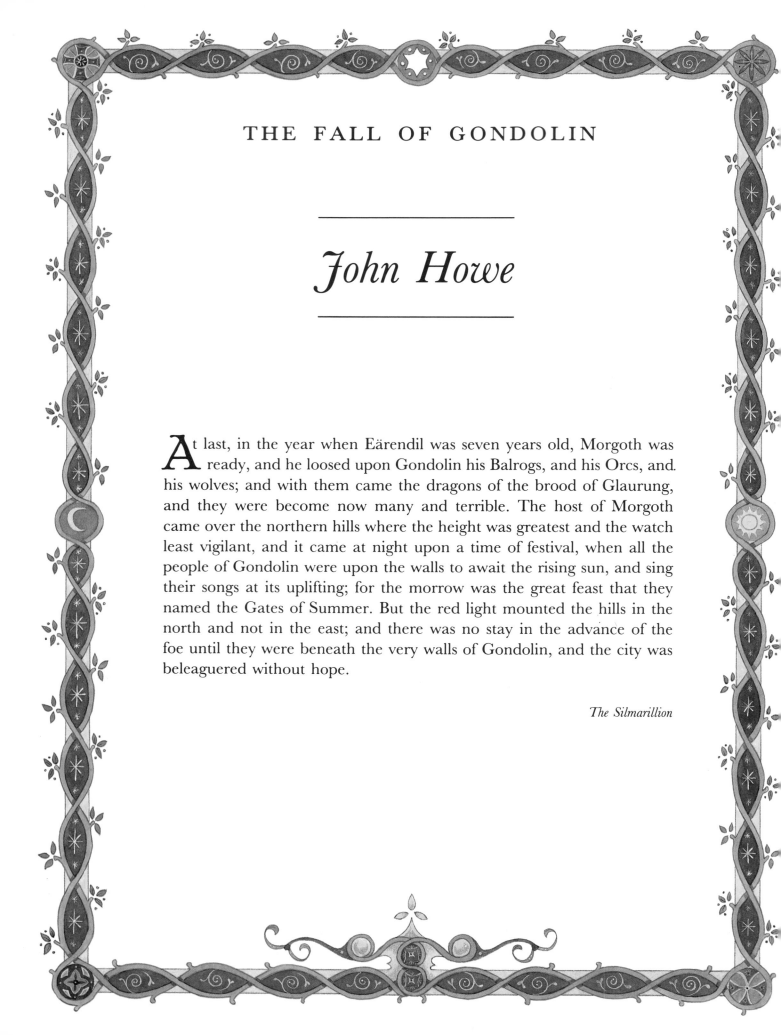

THE FALL OF GONDOLIN

John Howe

At last, in the year when Eärendil was seven years old, Morgoth was ready, and he loosed upon Gondolin his Balrogs, and his Orcs, and his wolves; and with them came the dragons of the brood of Glaurung, and they were become now many and terrible. The host of Morgoth came over the northern hills where the height was greatest and the watch least vigilant, and it came at night upon a time of festival, when all the people of Gondolin were upon the walls to await the rising sun, and sing their songs at its uplifting; for the morrow was the great feast that they named the Gates of Summer. But the red light mounted the hills in the north and not in the east; and there was no stay in the advance of the foe until they were beneath the very walls of Gondolin, and the city was beleaguered without hope.

The Silmarillion

EARENDIL AND ELWING

Roger Garland

Too late the ships of Círdan and Gil-galad the High King came hasting to the aid of the Elves of Sirion; and Elwing was gone, and her sons. Then such few of the people as did not perish in the assault joined themselves to Gil-galad, and went with him to Balar; and they told that Elros and Elrond were taken captive, but Elwing with the Silmaril upon her breast had cast herself into the sea.

Thus Maedros and Maglor gained not the jewel; but it was not lost. For Ulmo bore up Elwing out of the waves, and he gave her the likeness of a great white bird, and upon her breast there shone as a star the Silmaril, as she flew over the water to seek Eärendil her beloved. On a time of night Eärendil at the helm of his ship saw her come towards him, as a white cloud exceeding swift beneath the moon, as a star over the sea moving in strange course, a pale flame on the wings of storm.

The Silmarillion

THE DEATH OF GLAURUNG

Inger Edelfeldt

There she saw the dragon lying, but she heeded him not, for a man lay beside him; and she ran to Turambar, and called his name in vain. Then finding that his hand was burned she washed it with tears and bound it about with a strip of her raiment, and she kissed him and cried on him again to awake. Thereat Glaurung stirred for the last time ere he died, and he spoke with his last breath, saying: 'Hail, Nienor, daughter of the Húrin. We meet again ere the end. I give thee joy that thou hast found thy brother at last. And now thou shalt know him: a stabber in the dark, treacherous to foes, faithless to friends, and a curse unto his kin, Túrin son of Húrin! But the worst of all his deeds thou shalt feel in thyself.'

Then Glaurung died, and the veil of his malice was taken from her, and she remembered all the days of her life.

The Silmarillion

THE GATES OF MORN

Roger Garland

In the East however was the work of the Gods of other sort, for there was a great arch made, and, 'tis said, 'tis all of shining gold and barred with silver gates, yet few have beheld it even of the Gods for the wealth of glowing vapours that are often swathed about it. Now the Gates of Morn open also before Urwendi only, and the word she speaks is the same that she utters at the Door of Night, but it is reversed.

So it comes that ever now, as the Ship of the Moon leaves his haven in the East and his gates of pearl, Ulmo draws the galleon of the Sun before the Door of Night. Then speaks Urwendi the mystic word, and they open outward before her, and a gust of darkness sweeps in but perishes before her blazing light; and the galleon of the Sun goes out into the limitless dark, and coming behind the world finds the East again.

The Book of Lost Tales
VOLUME ONE

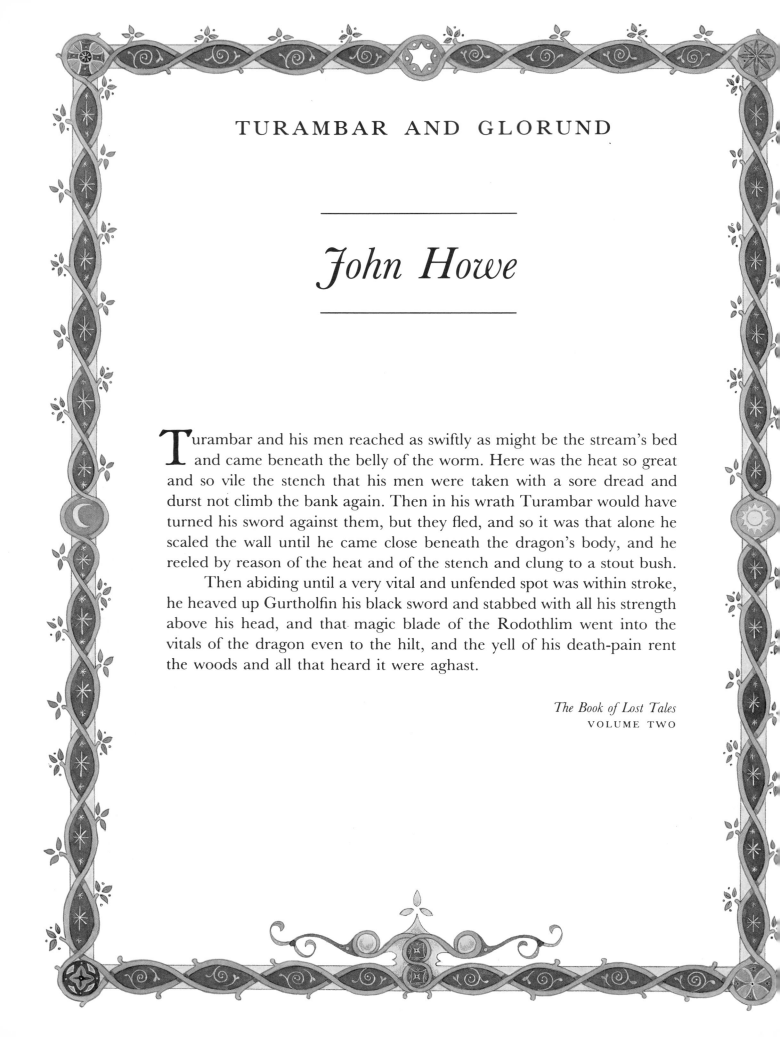

TURAMBAR AND GLORUND

John Howe

Turambar and his men reached as swiftly as might be the stream's bed and came beneath the belly of the worm. Here was the heat so great and so vile the stench that his men were taken with a sore dread and durst not climb the bank again. Then in his wrath Turambar would have turned his sword against them, but they fled, and so it was that alone he scaled the wall until he came close beneath the dragon's body, and he reeled by reason of the heat and of the stench and clung to a stout bush.

Then abiding until a very vital and unfended spot was within stroke, he heaved up Gurtholfin his black sword and stabbed with all his strength above his head, and that magic blade of the Rodothlim went into the vitals of the dragon even to the hilt, and the yell of his death-pain rent the woods and all that heard it were aghast.

The Book of Lost Tales
VOLUME TWO

Roger Garland

His father was a smith, and he followed him in his craft and bettered it. Smithson he was called while his father was still alive, and then just Smith. For by that time he was the best smith between Far Easton and the Westwood, and he could make all kinds of things of iron in his smithy. Most of them, of course, were plain and useful, meant for daily needs: farm tools, carpenters' tools, kitchen tools and pots and pans, bars and bolts and hinges, pot-hooks, fire-dogs, and horse-shoes, and the like. They were strong and lasting, but they also had a grace about them, being shapely in their kinds, good to handle and to look at.

But some things, when he had time, he made for delight; and they were beautiful, for he could work iron into wonderful forms that looked as light and delicate as a spray of leaves and blossom.

The Smith of Wootton Major

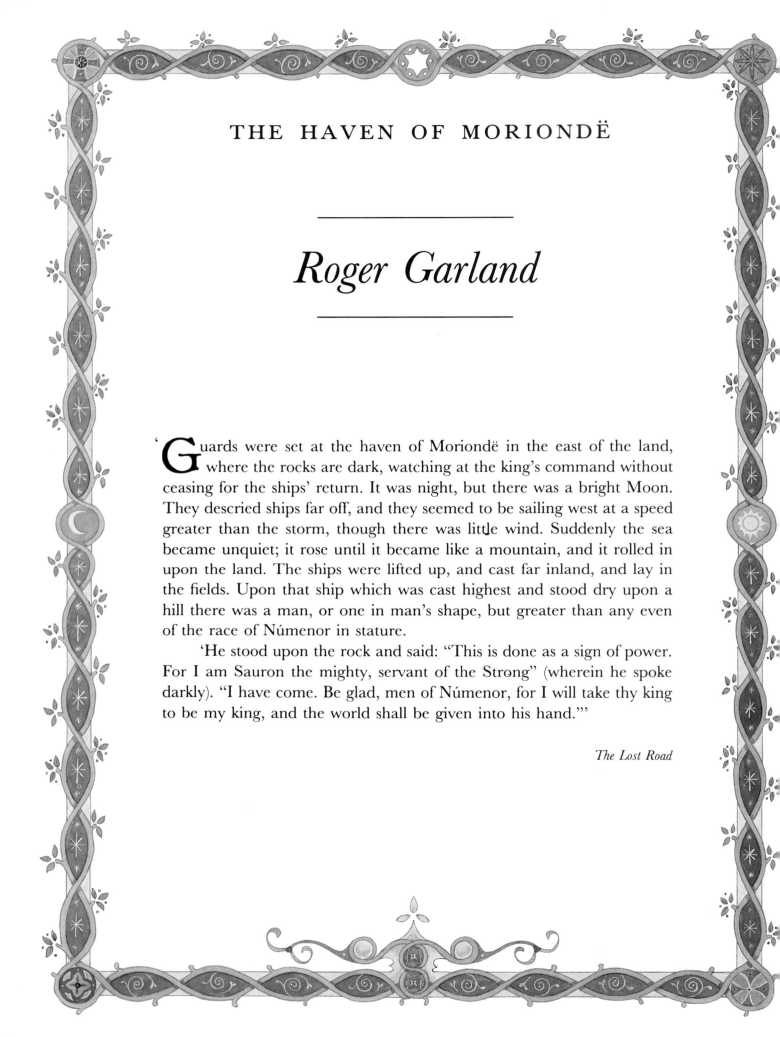

THE HAVEN OF MORIONDË

Roger Garland

'Guards were set at the haven of Moriondë in the east of the land, where the rocks are dark, watching at the king's command without ceasing for the ships' return. It was night, but there was a bright Moon. They descried ships far off, and they seemed to be sailing west at a speed greater than the storm, though there was little wind. Suddenly the sea became unquiet; it rose until it became like a mountain, and it rolled in upon the land. The ships were lifted up, and cast far inland, and lay in the fields. Upon that ship which was cast highest and stood dry upon a hill there was a man, or one in man's shape, but greater than any even of the race of Númenor in stature.

'He stood upon the rock and said: "This is done as a sign of power. For I am Sauron the mighty, servant of the Strong" (wherein he spoke darkly). "I have come. Be glad, men of Númenor, for I will take thy king to be my king, and the world shall be given into his hand."'

The Lost Road

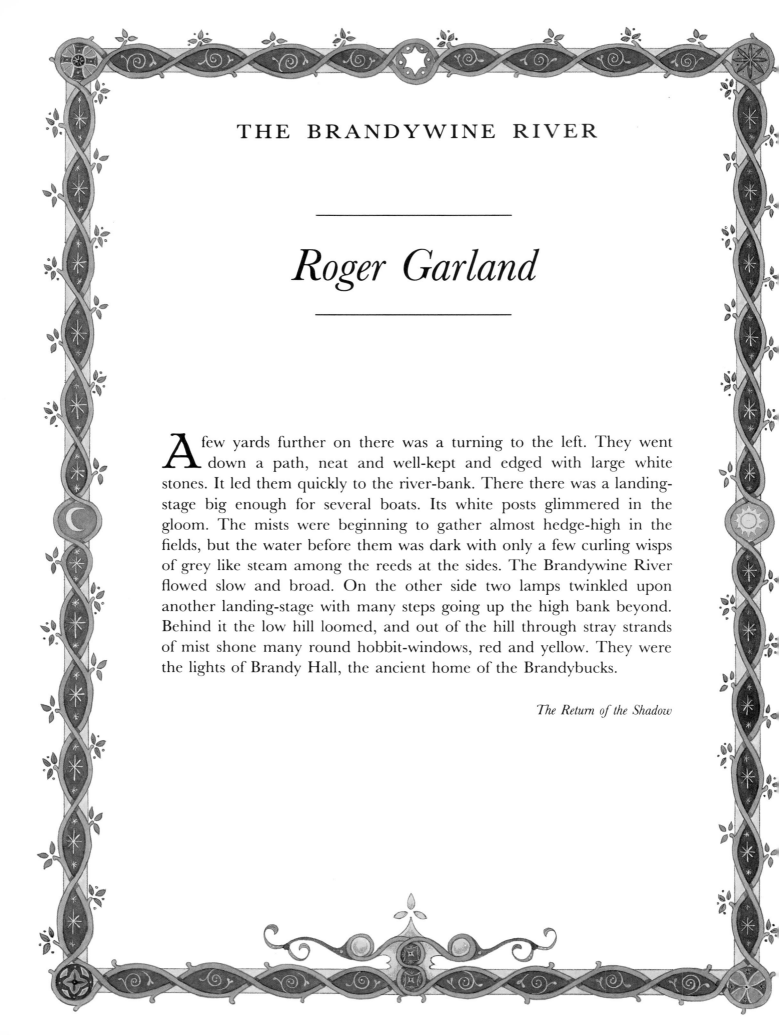

THE BRANDYWINE RIVER

Roger Garland

A few yards further on there was a turning to the left. They went down a path, neat and well-kept and edged with large white stones. It led them quickly to the river-bank. There there was a landing-stage big enough for several boats. Its white posts glimmered in the gloom. The mists were beginning to gather almost hedge-high in the fields, but the water before them was dark with only a few curling wisps of grey like steam among the reeds at the sides. The Brandywine River flowed slow and broad. On the other side two lamps twinkled upon another landing-stage with many steps going up the high bank beyond. Behind it the low hill loomed, and out of the hill through stray strands of mist shone many round hobbit-windows, red and yellow. They were the lights of Brandy Hall, the ancient home of the Brandybucks.

The Return of the Shadow

ABOUT
THE
ARTISTS

Inger Edelfeldt

I was born in Stockholm, Sweden – where I still live – in 1956. I am self taught, and besides being a book illustrator I have also been a professional writer since 1977. My books range from picture books for small children to novels and short stories for adults. In 1988 and 1989 I also published two comic books for adults.

When I was fourteen years old I read Tolkien's *The Lord of the Rings*. It made a great impact and inspired me very much. At sixteen, I painted my first series of watercolours depicting scenes, or rather persons, taken from Tolkien's works. It was very probably the contrast between good and evil, light and dark, ghostly wasteland and idyll that inspired me most. One of my favourite characters was, and has remained, Gollum. I've also tried, many times, to illustrate the elves, but they always came out looking like marble statues with eyes like glass beads and hair like sculpted caramel custard. The Orcs were another problem. What did they really look like?

In 1977, when I had just started working as a professional illustrator, I illustrated the covers for a new Swedish edition of *The Lord of the Rings*. In 1982 I met Mr Rayner Unwin (of George Allen & Unwin) in Stockholm. He looked at my pictures and some time later it was agreed that I should deliver 12 watercolours for the 1985 edition of the Tolkien Calendar. By then, Legolas the Elf had turned into some kind of palish Indian and the Orcs were burnt, rubbery, grey-black creatures with red eye slits and piggy noses.

One funny fact about the calendar is that when I needed a model, I used myself or friends. A very sweet, smallish and kindlooking female friend posed for all the slaughtered Orcs of "The Death of Boromir", for example. I myself, grimacing in front of a mirror, posed for Gollum. That was great fun, as I remember it. Good old Gollum got his fisssssh.

Carol Emery Phenix

I was born and grew up in Manchester, New Hampshire, USA and for the last ten years have made my home in the White Mountains of New Hampshire.

My first "illustrative experience" came at the age of 7 while listening to story readings every afternoon at school. Those afternoons were golden. Though I never actually drew any of my imaginings as the stories were read to us I can still remember how vividly I pictured those animal characters playing out their adventures in the sunny reeds by the river or in the dappled forest glades. Since that time I have always found my most artistic satisfaction is in the giving of life and breath to that which lies in the imagination, rather than just in the interpretation of reality.

At the age of 15 I happened to see a rather surrealistic television production of *A Midsummer Night's Dream*. That was my first "post-childhood" introduction to fantasy, and I was immediately attraced to its "Faërie-like" quality. I hungered for more, but at that time I was not aware that a whole genre of adult fantasy literature even existed. I remember drawing pictures of Oberon, Titania and especially Puck.

A year later I was introduced to JRR Tolkien's *The Hobbit* and *The Lord of the Rings*. The complexity of Middle-earth; the exactness of detail used in its description; its allusions to times and events and persons of importance outside the main story; the completeness of its cosmology; and especially that intangible "Northern" atmosphere all served to completely enthrall me. I was one of those fans who read the series over and over, each time finding new elements to savour, like a complex painting. In recent years I have become more attuned particularly to Tolkien's interweaving of his moral thinking into the fabric of his tale. His characters especially seem to be defined chiefly by their moral stature: the consummate evil of Sauron, the blindly horrible Balrog, tempted and wavering Boromir who falls but overcomes in the end; the mature, developed, clear-thinking Aragorn; and finally the refinement of Frodo into a person of such moral insight as to approach sanctity. Though idealised, I love them all.

The Lord of the Rings still holds incredible power for me, even after a 22 year aquaintance. I shall never tire of illustrating Tolkien.

Tony Galuidi

Mythologies have always drawn me. As a child I was fascinated by such gruesome creatures as the gorgons and hydra of Greek mythology and as I grew older I was moved more by the heroism, dignity, tragedy and beauty that most mythologies contain. Most inspiring to me are the grim, fierce tales of Norse mythology and the sadness and gallantry of Arthurian legend – hence my great love of Tolkien's writings which contain powerful elements of both.

I first read *The Lord of the Rings* about ten years ago and no book has moved me so profoundly – so rich it is with dignity and power, so full of hope and heroism. The characters and places within the book are so vibrant and potent that they virtually leap onto the artist's canvas – Barad-dûr in particular demands attention and no creature has captured my imagination like the dreadful Balrog of Khazad-dûm.

I am a self taught and relative newcomer to painting, having only begun five years ago, and I have very little time to paint due to work and family commitments. I work alongside adults with a learning difficulty at a training centre in Skelton, Cleveland which I find very rewarding and when I go home I have two 'wonderfully energetic' (!) children to contend with – Bethany who is four and shows great artistic tendencies and Joey who is two and shows only great 'demonic' tendencies.

Like most artists I have a deep reservoir of creative impressions and inspirations from which to draw. Tennyson's Arthurian epic *The Idylls of the King* continually rouses me as does the Anglo-Saxon poem *Beowulf*. For me the Victorians are the last word in painting and I admire the work of the Pre-Raphaelite painter, Waterhouse above all other artists. Other artists I greatly admire are Alphonse Mucha, Arthur Rackham, Patrick Woodroffe, Rodney Matthews and the moody and evocative work of Alan Lee (who was I believe born to illustrate *The Lord of the Rings*).

When I am not painting I play my flute or guitar (with more enthusiasm than ability) and best of all I love to walk in the woods or on the moors armed with nothing more than several of my favourite poems and a pair of wellies.

Roger Garland

I first read *The Hobbit* and *Lord of the Rings* as an art student in the late Sixties. At that time one could not escape its popularity and influence on a whole generation. I was thrilled ten years later to be commissioned to illustrate the cover for *Unfinished Tales*, in which I had the first opportunity to draw a dragon – Glaurung's destructive exit from his lair created an instant mental picture. I drew him straight from my imagination needing no reference. Recently I bought a first edition of *The Ring of the Nibelung*, illustrated by Arthur Rackham, and was surprised at the similarity between my Glaurung and Rackham's Fafner. There was no way I had seen it before yet they seemed to stem from a collective, mythical source handed down from one generation of illustrator to another.

From that initial commission I was asked to illustrate other covers for the Tolkien titles. I found *The Silmarillion*, *Unfinished Tales* and *Lost Tales* full of inspiration. It was from those books that I found powerful images like *Ulmo Lord of the Waters*, *The Chaining of Melkor*, and *The Tale of the Sun and the Moon*, which were first published in the 1984 Tolkien Calendar.

As artists the Pre-Raphaelites and French Symbolist painters inspired me the most. I was drawn to them firstly for their painting style, which was highly finished and incredibly detailed, and secondly for their mythical and fantastic subject. In their paintings you can find great beauty contrasting a darker, more threatening spiritual side, which I found had great similarities to Tolkien's works. Coupling the two sources of inspiration it was not difficult for me to develop a style of illustration to suit *Tolkien's World*. *The Lord of the Nazgûl* I think is my most successful illustration, incorporating both landscape and beast, and capturing the darker side of Tolkien's work.

Being involved in illustrating *Tolkien's World* over the past decade has allowed me to develop as an artist. For each painting I seemed to 'raise my game' and create something that was very special to me, and for that I am greatly indebted.

Robert Goldsmith

I was born and brought up in my home town of Brighton, being one of a family of six brothers!

I studied illustration at Brighton Polytechnic and graduated in June 1980 with B.A. (Hons) in Graphic Design. After leaving Brighton, I worked in London for several years before moving to Cheltenham in 1986.

It is the rich atmosphere and wonderful descriptions in Tolkien's work that stir my imagination and provide me with an irresistible urge to put pencil and brush to paper and try to reproduce some of the images that grow inside my head.

To want to illustrate a fictional world you have to believe in it. Tolkien has managed to create a place so real that it could almost be describing a parallel world which exists alongside our own. Indeed the people, places and powers in his created world of Middle-earth seem to me to be alike, in many respects, to those of our own.

The most successful illustrations that I have seen are those which do not portray the central characters in too much detail but instead rely on atmosphere and selective detail rather than meticulous definition, thus leaving a lot to the viewer's imagination and interpretation. I greatly admire the work of Alan Lee whose illustrations, I feel, fall into this category.

I've always worked as a freelance illustrator. Recently I have been spending an increasing amount of time on my own special interest: watercolour painting. Many a contented hour is spent travelling the Cotswolds on my motorbike in search of inspirational subject matter, heavy laden with stool, paints, brushes and sketchbooks.

My first one-man exhibition of water-colours was held at the Montpellier Gallery in June 1991, which will hopefully lead to further exhibitions in the future.

Michael Hague

I count myself as one of the most fortunate of beings for as an artist I have not only the pleasure but the duty to daydream. It is part of my work. I have been a contented daydreamer all my life, often to the the exasperation of those around me.

I strive to create something from an empty page that becomes a whole other world that people can visit for a while and totally believe in. It doesn't matter what type of project I'm working on, my approach is the same: to try to blend fantasy with reality.

Perhaps that explains why Tolkien's work has had such a great impact on my art. Tolkien's fantasy is based on reality. His world is one to which we can relate because we know the land, the trees, and the water. None of these things are alien despite the fact that the world they inhabit is mythical. Tolkien's beings – be they man, hobbit or goblin – are a part of us. We recognize the characters and their emotions because they are like ourselves.

The secret of J. R. R. Tolkien's success is that his fantasies are real. Perhaps they never happened or never could happen, but in our minds they strike a strong chord with what is and what could be.

Tolkien's world exists in our hearts and imaginations. I've tried my best to bring his world to life.

John Howe

Illustrating the works of J. R. R. Tolkien means deciding what is best not illustrated, deciding what needs deep shadow or distance or slanting November light. Tolkien is the master of evocation – his descriptions are catalysts for the reader, who summons his own personal pantheon of heroes and demons to complete the picture. Illustrating Tolkien means confronting these nebulous certitudes, radically differing from one reader to the next.

Illustrating Tolkien means treading warily, dipping one's brushes in shadow and rinsing them in light. Battle and balance, down the impossible path between the clear and the obscure.

Somewhat shamefacedly I am obliged to admit that I first read *The Two Towers* and *The Return of the King*, and finally *The Fellowship of the Ring*. I believe I was 12 or so at the time (I had read *The Hobbit* several years before), and the road to higher fantasy was only to be reached through the shelves of a small town public library.

Thus, I plunged directly into the world of Tolkien just above *The Falls of Rauros* and have been swimming diligently ever since.

Alan Lee

My chief concern in illustrating *The Lord of the Rings* was in attempting to provide a visual accompaniment for the story without interfering with, or dislodging, the pictures the author is carefully building up in the reader's mind. I felt that my task lay in shadowing the heroes on their epic quest, often at a distance, closing in on them at times of heightened emotion but avoiding trying to re-create the dramatic high points of the text.

One of the strongest images, for me, is that of Gollum dancing on the edge of the Crack of Doom with Frodo's severed finger in his hand, but it was the very vividness of that scene which deterred me from with wishing to depict it. (I preferred to try to capture the looming presence of Mount Doom itself, a few pages earlier, with Gollum watching the travellers from behind a rock; believing that if, as I hoped, the reader's impression of the volcano was strengthened then the subsequent events inside it could be even more powerful.)

Such considerations were made simpler by technical ones. Printed separately on a coated art paper, the pictures had to be positioned at intervals of sixteen or thirty-two pages throughout the book. This limitation was received gratefully and probably saved weeks of fruitless agonizing over which moments to illustrate.

It was important that every picture should be relevant to the text on the opposite page. It also suited my inclination towards finding subjects in some of the less obvious places.

It is such a rich work though that there are few, if any, pages in which something dramatic, wonderful or terrifying is not happening somewhere – and passages so beautiful and elegiac that any attempts to make them visible seem clumsy by comparison.

Tolkien succeeded in creating a world which exists beyond the scope of his own narrative. By establishing such a powerfully imagined landscape, and firm foundations of history and myth, he has made Middle-earth available to all of us for our own imaginative wanderings.

I feel immensely privileged to have been allowed to illustrate *The Lord of the Rings*, a book which has a profound impact on first reading and which has probably influenced the direction of my career over the following twenty-five years. It steered me, not towards fantasy, but to an invigorated interest in myth and legend, and a lifelong appreciation of the wonderful skills of the storyteller.

Ted Nasmith

Ted Nasmith lives and works in Toronto, Canada, where with his wife Donna he is raising three children, Colin, Michael and Sharyn. As an illustrator he divides his time between architectural rendering and a variety of other forms of illustration, particularly the Tolkien paintings he is becoming renowned for. Among several other interests are a love of songwriting, singing and recording, and of books: "There are an overwhelming number of good ones."

His love of Tolkien inspired him to create illustrations from the first reading of *The Lord of the Rings* at age fifteen. He was soon embarking on ambitious, detailed interpretations of scene after scene from the book, while accumulating a body of sketches. The first major piece was entitled "The Unexpected Party" (1972), rendered in tempera. It featured Gandalf, Bilbo and the dwarves examining the ancient map of Erebor. With encouragement he continued to turn out Tolkien illustrations on his own time for over a decade, some of which were to take many months to finish: particularly "Rivendell", a minutely detailed grand landscape that, according to the artist, is his "amplification" of Tolkien's own watercolour of the same name. In time his work was brought to the attention of George Allen & Unwin Ltd. and was soon being published in the Tolkien Calendars (1987, 1988, 1990 and 1992).

Says Nasmith: "When I began trying to illustrate Tolkien, I felt utterly at home with it, and followed my need to express this world, this story, and discover the essence of it all though my interpretations. I discovered much of my identity, ironically, by becoming a sort of conduit for visual expression of Tolkien's masterpiece. It chose me as much as I came to own it. The sadness, bittersweetness, darkness, light, glory, mystery and grandeur appeal to me. Similarly, the breadth and depth, the authenticity, the nobility, and maybe, overall, the wonder and 'northernness' as C. S. Lewis knew. Mine is a child's delight at having a gift, like Tolkien's love of language and story, which can communicate deeply with others of kindred spirit.